The Match That Lit the Fuse

Poems

Ashley L V Smith

Second Edition

For the inspirational people
who taught me to love writing
and to keep writing

Eileen Swigg
Peg Hulse
Hilary Barker
&
Kevin Jones

CONTENTS

THE MATCH THAT LIT THE FUSE

"You are only young once, but you can stay immature indefinitely."

— Ogden Nash

"...we should be careful
Of each other, we should be kind
While there is still time."

— from "The Mower" by Philip Larkin

The Mower

After Philip Larkin

The mower conked out. On close inspection, I found
That it had just run out of petrol. Having refilled
With a funnel, I pumped the choke three times

As per the instructions. It started first time
And I was back underway, circumnavigating
Tree trunks, dodging daffodils past their prime.

I didn't even see a hedgehog, let alone
Kill one. But then I'm not so busy writing poems
That I let the grass grow two feet high.

I may not be a poet. But at least I can mow a lawn
Without slaughtering the wildlife.

Blackbirds

We have watched them work through the final frosts
Colouring the branches with their shining calls,
Bright budburst notes wrapped tight and green as moss.

We never saw their eggs, stayed far away
Through the mother's brooding. With one still eye
She watched us working, till the fourteenth day.

And as we mowed, they came with full-stuffed bills,
To perch, heads cocked, above the squirming nest.
Mouths reached out and wide like daffodils.

Now the nest is empty. The work is done.
And as we mow the lawn again, they sit
In branches, singing green songs in the sun.

THE MATCH THAT LIT THE FUSE

The Gap in the Hedge

Some sheep always find the gap in the hedge
And dip into the lane to nibble dock.
Freed from the field, they find a better place
Of open hills and pastures with no end.

Exploring, they go onward, round the bend,
Then looking back there's no familiar face.
Spooked, they trot back home to join the flock,
Forget they'd ever ventured to the edge.

This Garden

This garden sings out to the world in green,
Tremolo leaves punctuating the air.
New movements swell from the soil to declare:
"We are here, where we always have been."

Each colour of sound that these flowers are giving -
The F sharps of yellow and B flats of blue -
They sing without pausing for breath, all on cue,
Almost exhausted from the joy of living.

THE MATCH THAT LIT THE FUSE

Galena

I don't know why the coal is different here:
Never the crackle of our fractious coalite
But the easy licking of a tongue
Shining every ember amber.

I am driving Corgi cars around carpet swirls,
Michael Foot above me on the screen,
Shouting something, Einstein hair flying.
Mrs Thatcher stares back from *The Daily Mirror*,
Unmoved,
With her helmet of curls.

Then the tapdance of too many keys
And Granddad's at the frosted door,
Streetlight sodium framing his shadow,
Pylons slicing the night behind.
'Here, have this...' as I run for my hug.
'Found it down't pit.'

He drops it like ten pence into my small pink hand
With his big bad one,
The one that was mangled in a machine
Before I was born.

Galena:
Star of the Usborne Spotter's guide (page 9).
I know its squareness instantly:
A cloud designed in Etch-a-Sketch lines
And built in Lego bricks of lead
Heavier than Derbyshire morning rain.

Its every facet speaks to me
Of outer space,
Of places I will never go.
I lose myself in it
As Granddad does in dinner with his dancing fork
Singly focused on the matter at hand.

THE MATCH THAT LIT THE FUSE

I roll this comet round my palm for hours
Caressing every edge,
Each keen-eyed corner,
As Grandma deftly darns a sock
And Granddad, with whisky and orange squash,
Turns Arthur Scargill up.

Gardeners' Question Time

"My leeks, my shamrock, my thistles and roses
Are no longer thriving," our listener discloses.
"What can I do to ensure they'll grow freely?
The answer should be inexpensive, ideally."
"May I ask firstly what else you have growing?
And which way is the prevailing wind blowing?"
"I've walls on all sides, so no hint of a breeze
And to keep it all tidy, I've cut down the trees.
I've dug up all species that aren't from these shores:
Tomatoes, potatoes and black hellebores
I just want my British plants richer and fuller
So I've driven out all of the non-native colour."
"Well, there is your problem, I'm sorry to say.
You're turning your soil into hard, sterile clay.
With only four species within your four walls
You'll soon find your fragile fertility falls.
The answer is simple: to get a rich loam
You just have to make it a welcoming home."

THE MATCH THAT LIT THE FUSE

Economic Downturn

After Percy Bysshe Shelley

I met a tat seller at The Antiques Land
Who said—"Two cracked and lidless jugs I own
Sit here both for sale... Also this inkstand
Of mine, whose shattered glass of turquoise tone
And sticky label - 'Made in Sunderland' -
Might tempt you to invest in it instead.
As if alive, here gleam these gorgeous things
This Queen Mum mug, this lava lamp in red."
And in a picture frame these words appear:
You'll haggle in vain, even if that stings.
Look at my prices, ye buyers, and despair!
A pile of crap remains. A brass ashtray,
A Skegness spoon... Whichever way you stare,
The customerless stands stretch far away.

Song For Those Who Don't Complain

After Wilfred Owen

They listen. They do not raise a question
To the announcer's pacifying prattle.
Street-lame, nostrils charged with congestion,
They have the time to spare to stare. Strange cattle
Swaying with sandwiches, numbered tickets;
Patient to join the pay-per-viewers,
To oh-well the early loss of wickets,
A nation of shoppers, silent queuers.

On Sundays, when we get the mower out,
That ticklish sweetness speaks of ancient walks
Along riverbanks, with Grandfather's tales
Of Victory, of Glory that never pales.
We jab the rusty blades with garden forks.
We are tired. Not much else to moan about.

Worries

They turn up like buses, too often in threes,
As if they know you are stood there waiting,
Coatless, exposed to the critical breeze.
They turn up like buses, too often in threes,
Suddenly looming through cobwebs of trees.
Then you climb onboard, unhesitating.
They turn up like buses, too often in threes
As if they know you are stood there waiting.

Hymn for TV executives

Make me a channel of your peace
With none of those adverts for *GoCompare*
Just Alan Bennett plays and *Gardener's World*,
And lots of old repeats of *Countryfile*.

Oh, Master, grant that I may never see
Anything involving clubs in Ibiza,
Total Wipeout, TOWIE or *Celeb BB*
And absolutely no Jeremy Kyle.

Make me a channel of your peace,
Where there is *BGT*, give me *Countdown*
Where there's *X Factor*, give me *Sky At Night*,
And where there's *Love Island*, just give me *Coast*.

Oh, Master, grant that I may never see
Stuff to do with ASBOs and tattoo regrets,
Documentaries dealing with binge-drinking teens
Or any programme that Ant and Dec host.

Make me a channel of your peace
With nothing that resembles *Final Score*.
Bring back *Bagpuss, Brideshead, Bergerac*
And steal the *Bake-Off* back from Channel 4.

The Elephant in the Room

Inspired by 'Countdown' by Alan Weisman

We welcomed it in as an infant:
It seemed very cute way back when.
But now it's a grey brutish giant,
It's a bit late to think: Think again.

Its bulk has spilled out to each corner
And it's damaged each table and chair.
The whole room feels stiflingly warmer
Like it's breathing the last of the air.

And after it's cleaned out the larder,
And its trunk has drunk everything dry,
And it's left us neck-deep in its ordure
Still then we won't ask ourselves why.

Only when walls all start falling,
The whole house rocks on its foundation,
And even the elephant's bawling...
Then we'll discuss population.

Situations Vacant

Following the resignation of Tim Farron as leader of the Lib Dems

We're looking for a leader, since the former leader's quit
And we really need somebody who will be a perfect fit:
A candidate who's fully Democratic to the letter
(And if you are a Liberal than that would be even better).

Dear Applicant, please heed our firm and sensible advice:
If you're not that tolerant, you maybe should think twice.
Our leader must be fully signed up for equality,
So if that piques your conscience, why not join the DUP?

If you're rather troubled by what others do in bed,
They're crying out for vicars. Why not go do that instead?
It's really not that relevant who is and isn't sinning.
What we need is someone with an appetite for winning.

THE MATCH THAT LIT THE FUSE

Number 12

Today I drove to the magistrates
Under wet newspaper skies
To find out if this is really what I want to do,
To decide the future of those
Whose present is drenched in past.

Sheep in fields along the way
Had new company. A pair of lambs,
Or just the one, following, nuzzling.
Mother and offspring number-matched
To help in the event of loss.

Number 12 and her trembling twins
Grazed right beside the gate where I stopped,
Aware but untroubled.
Mother kept them carefully close,
Little twelves stumbling in the warmth of her wake.

Later at court, Case 12 shuffled into the dock,
Hollow-eyed, gently prodded into place.
The prosecutor listed things:
"Possession of a bladed article..."
The defence then listed things back.

She had long left home and the fists and the kicks.
Sleeping now in a borrowed tent.
Friends, but none to offer a fixed abode.
Only cider to sluice the memories away.
She sat impassively watching the wall.

Refusing all help, probation explained.
Unwilling to change, at least for now.
Better to leave her to find her own way.
The bench agreed: Suspended sentence,
Weak words of warning. She nodded and left.

I stopped at the same gate
On the road back home. Number 12 stood there,

THE MATCH THAT LIT THE FUSE

Untouched by time. Her lambs stumbled, stop-start,
A few feet away.
They did not leave her gathering gaze.

The Day that Donald Trump Dies

The sun will still rise
And somewhere clouds will rain.
Light will seep through the cracks
Of the morning.
Again.

Lilies on ponds will open whitely,
Brainless,
Exposed to the unseeing sky,
Painless.

Fish will spiral through oceans,
Unblinking
Or shimmer in bubbles of glass,
Unthinking.

Lions will doze beneath swoopings
Of finches
And dusk-gloom will deepen,
Unhindered,
By inches.

And they will know nothing
As they do their rising,
Their raining,
Their seeping and blooming,
Their swimming and dozing,
Their swooping,
Their glooming...

Over this better,
This ever so slightly better
Earth.

THE MATCH THAT LIT THE FUSE

Hospitals

Following a visit to Wenlock Priory

Hard to believe every city had one
Once, a hospital like this. (Medicine
Was considered valuable back then.)
Hospitals inspired awe, devotion.

Take a long look at these old foundations
Worn smooth by centuries of erosion.
This building served a huge population
Who thought it the best place to get well in.

These crumbling walls contained things they called 'wards'
For the ill - or 'patients' - as you may have heard
Them referred to. Now it seems quite absurd
That we'd give such care, let alone afford

The vast expanse. They were such wasteful times
Back then. Buildings of this enormous size
Cost a fortune. Debts rose, interest declined.
These monsters were bleeding the country dry.

People no longer sought medical help,
Ignored the outdated doctrines of health
And turned instead to the Cult of the Self:
What else matters, if you've still got your wealth?

Finally, they were all shut down by law
And now they just sit here for us to explore.
And children wonder, "Well, what were they for?"
Since nobody sickens or dies anymore.

THE MATCH THAT LIT THE FUSE

Cargoes

After John Masefield

South Korean freighter ploughing past Gibraltar
Heading on to Suez chasing tight deadlines
With a cargo of iPhones
Toys from Taiwan,
Cigarettes, Kalashnikovs and anti-tank mines.

Playboy yacht from Monaco gliding down to Malta
Taking Russian oligarchs for sun, sea, sand
With a cargo of cocaine,
Champagne, oysters,
Footballers, glamour girls and Russell Brand.

Leaky open fishing boat from lawless Libya
Limping on in vain to reach Italian shores
With a cargo of terrified
Shivering Syrians
Struggling for oxygen with sunburnt sores.

THE MATCH THAT LIT THE FUSE

Condition of the Sea
12 September 2017
Latitude: 44.346525   Longitude: 14.601731

Inspired by the Croatian weather service's English translation of the Douglas Scale

Yesterday, the sea was calm,
Not quite a zero mirror,
But 1: wrinkled with phenomena.

Today is mainly 2:
Short, small waves,
Shaped.
The banks look glassy.
But we are moving up to 3:
Places of whiteness here and there,
Intermittent rustling.

For 4, the noise must look
Like a mock clap.
Not quite there yet.
No waves with many whites.

Tonight, from the south, will come the pushing,
The thick white strips of 6,
Or 5:
Marine giant
Blowing off the foam
With its continuous clatter;
Its noise is like a whirling hook.

Then crumbling,
Creating coronation,
Foam flared from sparkling hills,
Waves rolling hard and striking:
7.

And back home,
Aileen is 8,
Cleaning the peaks of all the waves,

THE MATCH THAT LIT THE FUSE

The sea completely filled with sea smoke, stripes.

The waves cross each other
From different directions,
A complex interference impossible to describe.
Waves collapse
And heave
And wish,
Wish to look again
In the mirror.

Pulling the Perse Strings

For anyone who's ever been through the admissions process to The Perse Upper School, Cambridge

So, how has Tom been doing since the start of Autumn term?
He tells us he's been trying hard and we've been rather firm
About how much he's going on the internet at home
Except for when he's Skyping with a French boy called Guillaume.
We've tried to get him up for maybe doing an exchange
But Tom seems quite reluctant, which I'm finding very strange.
His appetite is dwindling and his sleep is getting worse,
So what we want to know is: is he on track for The Perse?

This latest comprehension test he did the other day
His tutor took him through it all and I'd just like to say
That Tom was really anxious that he'd got a lowish score:
He's used to getting ninety-plus and this was eighty-four.
He wants some more past papers just to put his mind at rest,
To boost his inner confidence so that he does his best.
D'you know whether the passage will be prose or be in verse?
Please tell us how to help him so he gets into The Perse.

The entrance tests are just around the corner and we think
That Tom will thrive on learning how to swim and not to sink.
All his friends are going there, he hates to be left out,
And academic rigour is what he cares most about.
He ought to pass the interview, and though we're loath to push,
Some practice questions would be great to help him not to blush
And while you're at it how about some answers to rehearse,
Since standards keep on rising for the entrance to The Perse?

Our biggest worry's Maths. *Tom, darling, wouldn't you agree?*
So the tutor's had him tackling things beyond GCSE.
(Sadly, I can't help him with his homework anymore.
I only got an A myself. I know! Terribly poor!)
In your opinion, have the extra sessions upped his grades
Or do we need to book some more and lay it on in spades?
Hard graft's a thing, you know, to which our Tom is not averse
And all he ever talks about is getting to The Perse!

THE MATCH THAT LIT THE FUSE

If he weren't to get a place there it would really be so cruel.
We just can't see him fitting in in any other school.
It's way up in the league tables and wonderfully near...
Sit up, Tom, and listen! It's for you that we're all here!
Oundle's gone too *nouveau riche* and Rugby's gone too rowdy
And if he goes to Eton then we'll have to swap the Audi.
Tom's heart is set, he's driven and it's too late to reverse,
The world will crash around us if he can't go to the Perse!

Parent Power

After Dylan Thomas

Do not be fearful of spoiling for a fight!
No matter what those dreadful teachers say.
Rage, rage that the marking isn't right.

The school has robbed those marks in broad daylight!
Just one mark lost is proof of dark foul play.
Do not be fearful of spoiling for a fight!

If the percentage doesn't match up quite
To what you had expected, don't give way:
Rage, rage that the marking isn't right.

Don't waste time bothering to be polite
You've earned the straight A stars for which you pay
Do not be fearful of spoiling for a fight!

Do they not understand your offspring's plight?
Such wrongs destroy one's life, not just one's day.
Rage, rage that the marking isn't right.

Injustice is the issue, not mere oversight
If they don't listen, if they won't obey,
Do not be fearful of spoiling for a fight!
Rage, rage that the marking isn't right.

Tiger Mother

After William Blake

Tiger Mother, quick to fight
For your precious child's birth right!
What mere mortal PhD
Is fit to teach your progeny?

With what wild, relentless fire
Will you cast injunctions dire
When sweetie fails to conjugate
His Latin at a given rate?

With what predatory claws
Do you pounce on Chopin scores?
What keen whiskers seek out those
Endless tough arpeggios?

And what if in his Physics test
He isn't top, he's second best?
Confiscate his new computer?
Drag in Brian Cox to tutor?

And how do you view other mums
Who do not dole out extra sums?
Is their laxness incorrect
Or tantamount to child neglect?

By what parents were you raised
To end up so completely crazed?
See your darling's downcast eye:
Did Larkin's warning pass you by?

And when he runs off to Australia,
On whose head be this ghastly failure?
Who will suffer, who will pay
Now that your cub has slunk away?

Tiger Mother, quick to fight

THE MATCH THAT LIT THE FUSE

For your precious child's birth right!
What mere mortal PhD
Dare teach your wondrous progeny?

THE MATCH THAT LIT THE FUSE

Privet Seller, Female Car

From an advert seen on Autotrader

Who will buy my lush green bushes?
Two shrubs for a tenner.
No, you won't find better hedging plants
Between here and Vienna.

It will help to keep the privacy
Of your semi in Leicester
You can rely on my integrity;
I'm a lady Ford Fiesta.

I'm not just glossy paint and curves
I'm cunning as a weasel.
I can advise on topiary:
Just fill me up with diesel.

Tumble Dryer

Inspired by a story in The Evening Sentinel

Mother speaks of terror when her tumble dryer broke:
"In less than thirty seconds the whole kitchen filled with smoke.
I never should have bought it from that dodgy-looking bloke.
The world must soon be ending if such things take place in Stoke."

The 747s

Dedicated to a plane-obsessed pupil

I wandered freely as a bird
That flies on high o'er Ghent and Metz
When all at once I saw and heard
A host, of silver jumbo jets,
On the tarmac, by the gate
Taxi-ing, ready to aviate.

Luxurious as the cars that shine
And twinkle on the motorway,
They stretched in never-ending line
By Heathrow airport's main runway:
At least ten had I in my sight
Thrust-reversing with all their might.

Package tourists neared, but they
Outdid the garish hordes in glee:
A pilot could no more delay
For such a drunken company.
I gazed ahead with cheery soul,
On high, in air traffic control.

Oft in departure lounge I sit,
In vacant or in pensive mood,
And watch the jumbos brightly lit,
Upon their aprons nobly queued;
Then my heart rises to the heavens,
And dances with 747s.

On the Eighth Day

For a philosophy lesson on colour

On the eighth day, God awoke, understood
Everything that he had created
And, once again, he saw that it was good

Each planet, porpoise, crocus and cascade -
Immaculately sculpted and defined
In wiry vines of liquid light and shade -

Was pure of form and yet still incomplete,
In need of a different heartbeat.

First he drew blue from the heart of a stone
With ice-brittle skin
Which he found on a mountain
Asleep, alone.

And then he squeezed green
From the crystalline fear of a solitary deer
Staring, still, silent,
Almost unseen.

Yellow was mined from the cave of the night
Where it hid,
Clutching claws,
In the blade of a stalactite

And he opened a canyon in Adam's head
To unleash a rolling river of dreams
Which he scooped up and bottled
As the very first red.

From the past he took black
From the future, white
And when he had finally filled the lack
He paused
Then gave us sight.

A Line That Still Hasn't Turned Into a Poem

The sky has hung its washing out to dry

Mirror World

Written in 1990 for Mrs Swigg, who got me writing

The clocks go back in time and lights
Stand upright from the peeling plastered floor
Like lamp posts.
Mirrors reflect
Mirrors within
Mirrors;
An eternal row of military images which vanish
Into the distance.
The room revolves,
Crashing ghostly figures into each other unawares.
The room is like a house of cards
Where Kings meet Queens in the middle
But face away.
Siamese Jacks, silently bisected and sewn together
In sudden operations.

In this mad world
The boys wear blouses and the girls wear shirts.
Extra-limbed aliens walk around as if human.
We read in a foreign alphabet
And write wrong-handed.
Then the mirror moves
And the House of Cards comes tumbling down.

Meeting

Another one for Mrs Swigg

I turn on the taps
And the steam hides my friend
Behind a misty opaque window
Of smoke.
The only way I can bring him back
Is to slap him
And to smear my fingers across
His cold and shapeless face.
So why doesn't he go away
Or even slap me back?

His glossy eyes give an icy stare
And his smile is faked.
His red face is washed
And his hair combed into strange contortions
Until we are complete.
Then we depart from the strange window,
To return some other time
That we both know,
But without a word spoken
Between us.

Ode to Maths

Written to cheer up some 11-year-olds prior to an end-of-year Maths exam

If teaching Maths was left to me
And I could make the rules,
I'd do it rather differently
From all the other schools.

First, I'd deal with numbers:
I'd have a big rethink.
I'd make all sevens tangerine
And fours would be bright pink.

Nines would smell of violets,
Fives would taste of cheese.
Hundreds would all be replaced
With velvet twenty-threes.

I'd weaken all the powers,
Set integers aflame.
I'd send back all the factors
To the factory whence they came.

Then I'd sort out tables
Because they're too much faff.
I'd chop them up with axes
Nicked from a scattergraph.

Lines and shapes I'd tinker with,
To wonderful effect.
I'd swing from a trapezium;
All angles would be wrecked.

I'd make all square roots curly
Make vectors disappear.
I'd scream till I was louder
Than the volume of a sphere.

To end, I'd bar all bar charts,

THE MATCH THAT LIT THE FUSE

Make everyone eat pi,
Then go forth on a tangent
And never multiply.

So there you have my big idea:
My mental acrobatics.
All it needs now is a name:
Yes! *Impure Mathematics!*

Anger

Written for a Year 3 poetry workshop on feelings

Anger stamped into the class,
Slammed back the black unhappy door.
He flung his satchel to the floor.
And smashed the air to flashing glass.

He kicked and writhed with flicking fire
And roared as hard as a warring wolf
Across a never-ending gulf.
His eyes steel-sharp, like white-hot wire.

He stormed and lurched from side to side
And glared half-blind with reddened rage,
But, like a tiger in its cage,
I kept my vengeance locked inside.

When Anger saw my cool, small calm,
The smiling boy with unclenched fists
He stepped back slow, through peace-filled mists
And fell asleep, in the drop of an arm.

THE MATCH THAT LIT THE FUSE

Antarctica

Written for a Year 2 poetry workshop

You may not have noticed me,
Minding my own business
Down here
At the bottom of the Earth
Like a speech bubble stuffed
With snowy silence...
Ignore me at your peril!
I can impale you on my ivory tusk.
In my cold, clutching claws
I can snatch the sneaky, summer sun
And stop him from slinking away.
Or I banish him north for many a month
And just keep my maiden,
The milky moon, for company.
And make her green fairies dance
In the garden of my mind.
I send out my warriors to scour the sea,
In defence of my kingdom,
Each one a bullet in search of a target.
While my strange ballerinas swirl their skirts in the darkness,
Trapped behind glass until I set them free.
I'll drop not one tear of pity
On my wind-parched valleys,
However loud they may howl.
And with the fire in my belly
I'll cough flames from deep down
To torment the terrified air.
I could chew you to pieces
With my tyrannosaur teeth.
Or rip you to ribbons
In one roar from my thundering throat.
Seas stand still at my command
And cower as they gaze up
At my glittering crown.
Yes, down here,
I am king.

THE MATCH THAT LIT THE FUSE

I have hidden depths.
Ignore me at your peril.
One of these days
I might be coming to get you...

Citius Altius Fortius

Written for a Year 4 poetry workshop on the Olympic Games

Swifter than a spark I was born,
A spark struck from a golden disc.
I shot down in a sudden stream from the highest heavens
And burst into life,
Kicking and screaming in my silver cradle.

Higher than the spotless sky
My mother gazed down at me
With a shimmering smile, flaming with pride
As they held me aloft,
Armoured in bronze.

Stronger than Hercules,
Heavy with heroism,
I surged through streets,
Scaled mountains,
Raced over raging rivers
And grew...

Until I arrived at the city gates,
Triumphant,
My destiny blazing.

Citius Altius Fortius.

Making Bread

After "The Lake Isle of Innisfree"

I will arise and grow now microbiotically
And a small loaf enliven, of wholemeal flour made.
I'll reproduce with vigour in my warm ecology
Emit CO_2 in the humid shade

W B Yeast

Anagrams

In each section, all lines are anagrams of each other. This is the kind of thing I used to do in staff meetings and still do in trains.

I wandered lonely as a cloud
And called on your wise lead.
Caledonia answered loudly
And our yellow ladies dance.

***

Shall I compare thee to a summer's day
Thou art more special, madam, else shy,
Clothed as a royal seraph. Mute mimes
Mar the malaise as the loud poems cry.

***

Had I the heavens' embroidered cloths,
As had demon lover the cherished bite,
Then I'd describe ahead, love, her moths.
Her odd bedsheets hover in malachite.

I would spread the cloths under your feet,
Drop four and tell you secrets hued white,
Then cupid the rudders of our yellow seat
And decode hero opuses, truthfully write.

***

47

THE MATCH THAT LIT THE FUSE

Twas brillig and the slithy toves
Both had twelve laryngitis lists
All shiny gilt the drab wit stoves
The hat got led by villain's wrists

***

She walks in beauty like the night
As blue as the light ye knew, I think.
Hunt a bleak eye with silken sight.
Betake healthy sigh until we sink.

***

Because I could not stop for Death,
I chose to operate on fat dud clubs;
And cheerful despots coo it about:
Acoustic flood on preheated tubs.

THE MATCH THAT LIT THE FUSE

To Bethlehem

Written for a Christmas Carol Service

"You must come now," they ordered by decree,
"To Bethlehem, to tell us who you are.
"The journey may be hard, it may be far,
But our taxation system has to be

Obeyed." The donkey shrugged and bowed his head
To take the bridle in his velvet mouth.
Then Mary, he and I, we headed south,
As eastern skies rose up blood-orange red.

The day was long and blue, still was the air.
A liquid sun forebode a frozen night.
Above us, one grey falcon's circling flight
Echoed one thought: Lord, get us safely there.

The west blew out the dying flick of fire
And left us trudging half-blind through the black
That curled around us. We did not look back.
Hunger held us close. Cold sang like a choir.

At last the town gleamed from the wide-eyed gloom.
Warmth seemed to seep from under each closed door.
We knocked, we called. I said, "Let's try one more."
Were we so wrong to think there might be room?

"There is an old stable," our saviour said.
Now Mary could lie down in straw on the ground.
The donkeys nodded, the cows made no sound,
Just welcomed us in and lent us a bed.

THE MATCH THAT LIT THE FUSE

Comet

Astronomers know they will see me again,
Threaded, friendless, on a skywire, my
Linen-tailed, silent slide-by.

Back then, I came around unannounced,
Surprising an entire hemisphere,
Who supposed me meaningfully here

To light a line to heaven knows what.
(I, of course, had been kept in the dark,
A glass bead strung on an iron arc

That had fixed my path since the black was born.)
Old follower, now followed, I
Sheepishly whitened a patch of sky,

Drew in a flock from grassless lands
And hovered, so it seemed, above
A byre, which sparsely sheltered a love

Foreseen for a thousand years.
Finally witnessed by cattle and men,
The momentary miracle shone. Then

The infant, like me, was spirited off
In bandages into a star-strewn domain,
But wise men know we will come again.

THE MATCH THAT LIT THE FUSE

Villanelle

The clock's slow ticks. Your heart's dry beat.
The telephone waits, indifferently dumb,
And endlessly the days and nights repeat.

Footsteps thump from the frozen street,
Fade to air like a passing drum.
"The clock's slow," ticks your heart's dry beat.

The fire gives off an unfelt heat,
The radio, a half-heard hum,
And endlessly the days and nights repeat.

One by one your hopes retreat,
As shadows on the floor become
The clock's slow tick, your heart's dry beat.

Pages snowdrift at your feet.
You stare them through, unreading, numb,
And endlessly. The days and nights repeat

Until their sameness is complete
And now you know I will not come.
The clocks, slow, tick your heart's dry beat
And, endlessly, the days and nights. (Repeat.)

Poetry Evening

Their firebright words lit up the air
In rhythmic reds and rhyming blues.
Unseen, she smiled to sit here where
She'd struck the match that lit the fuse.

Printed in Poland
by Amazon Fulfillment
Poland Sp. z o.o., Wrocław